YouTube Secret

Dean Alma   thebluecrusader

2023

Copyright

Copyright © 2023

by Dean Alma

Majorwolf Productions

Contents

Introduction 1

Laying the Foundation 4

Creating Compelling Content 11

Mastering the YouTube Algorithm 17

SEO: Thumbnails, Titles & Tags 22

Fostering a Loyal, Engaged Community 27

Monetizing Your YouTube Machine 32

The Long-Term Growth Strategy 38

Expanding Beyond YouTube 42

Overcoming Challenges 45

Conclusion 48

Introduction

You probably picked up this book because you want to become a YouTuber, right? Or maybe you just got a copy to support me, if you know me that is…

Perhaps you don't, so it's best we become acquainted.

My name is Dean, also known as "thebluecrusader", or Dean Alma if you know me from my personal brand. I'm excited that you chose to embark on your own journey to uncover the secrets behind success on YouTube. With over 100,000 subscribers and a number of years at this point under my belt, I am confident I can now speak from a position of authority. I've decided to share all my knowledge from my trials and tribulations, triumphs and many failures to help you navigate the ever-evolving world of YouTube.

From the moment I stumbled onto YouTube as a kid in 2007, it captivated me, mainly as an entertainment matrix, but then as a creative outlet. In 2008, I started making random videos just for fun, dabbling in stupid and silly videos, making memes and later, making crazy action videos in the garden, at my friend's houses or in the woods and editing cool explosions and effects on the computer. I've always been a film maker, and those days I was heavily inspired by Freddie Wong (FreddieW) and the guys at Corridor Digital.

In 2015, I started creating higher quality content, I was in college studying Film & TV production and I needed an outlet to express my creativity and passion for film, I was making Star Wars lore videos and gaming documentaries and commentaries, and some picked up some traction.

But it wasn't until a few years later, around 2018, where I started uploading videos and taking it seriously. I was posting up to 4 videos a day, mainly focusing on quantity over quality at many points, but it was a slow journey of growth, but as the money started to slowly drip in and the subscribers grew into a community, I was hooked.

Throughout this book, I'm going to share everything I've learnt from my personal journey as a YouTuber. I'm going to guide you through the ins and outs of navigating the platform and understanding the elusive YouTube algorithm, discuss the art of creating highly compelling content, and reveal my strategies that helped me reach the 100,000 subscriber milestone.

As you read deeper into this book, you'll learn about all my insights, tips and tricks that I've accumulated over the years, from thousands of hours of learning from videos, reading articles and books and the trial and error of creating, editing and producing more than 2,000 videos. This book is going to act as your mentor, I am your mentor, through the pages of this book, this is my blueprint to success, that will fast track you to the finish line, whilst avoiding the failures and hardships I had to experience to get to the success I have.

All of these proven and tested methods will help you navigate the ever-changing world of online video. You'll learn how to build up a solid foundation for your channel, optimizing it as well as your content for maximum chances of being discovered and learning how to connect with your audience in a way that builds trust and propels you to success.

But this book isn't just about the technical part of being a YouTube creator, we'll explore the personal side of the journey and how to maintain your creativity and overcome challenges along the way.

I'm confident that the lessons I'm going to teach you in this book will be invaluable to you, be it that you're just starting out or you're looking to elevate your YouTube game to a whole new level.

So, let the journey begin,

- Dean.

Laying the Foundation

Before you dive into creating your channel, it's essential that you begin to lay the building blocks to create a solid foundation, this will be your vision. This is going to be what will help you to stand out from the millions of content creators already out there. There's a lot of wannabes, grifters and general noise polluting the space, so you need to be different, or better. To do this, you need to choose your niche, define your target audience, and develop a unique and consistent format for your brand.

Picking a Niche

Your niche is basically the specific topic or theme that you are going to base your channel and videos off of. Choosing the right niche is crucial, this is because it will make or break your channel and it will make you stick to it during the hard times of the long process of growing if you genuinely like what you're making.

You can also connect with likeminded people that you will reach through creating targeted and engaging videos appealing to the people in your chosen niche.

You need to consider the following when you're deciding on what to create.

- **Passion** – What are you actually passionate about? If you have something you genuinely enjoy, creating content around it wouldn't be a bad idea. Following your passion can sometimes be a bad idea in business, but on YouTube, it makes sense.

- **Expertise** – What do you know a lot about? Or what are you actually good at? Try to choose a topic or space you have knowledge or experience in so you can become an authority to your future subscribers or fans.

- **Demand** – Is there an audience that already exists for your niche? You can do some market research by just searching through YouTube by using key words or search terms based around what you want to create in order to see if there's already successful creators making content in that topic.

Try to have a combination of the listed factors to have the best chance for success.

At first, you may not know exactly what kind of videos you want to create, you might have multiple interests and just want to make videos and trial and error will get you to where you want to be.

If you don't know yet whether you want to make gaming content, fitness videos or cooking shorts, then you could try experimenting with things until something works, then replicate the success by making more of it and niching down into what you're good at.

Not everyone will know what to do at the start, if you don't have that passion, chosen niche or interest, you can experiment, I like to call this the creator learning curve.

Just remember, just because you're passionate about something, doesn't mean you're good at it. You can either keep doing it to get good, or if you're already good at something, you can focus on that, remember, if you want to create a career as a content creator or generate some kind of revenue, you need to provide a lot of value, so you have to be good at what you're doing or be dedicated to get good.

Defining Your Target Audience

Once you figure out your niche or topic you want to double down into, you need to gauge an idea of what your audience is going to be and what they're going to look like. Your target audience is theoretically the specific group of people who are going to be most interested in your content, resonate with you, and be dedicated to your channel and mission. Having a clear idea and understanding of this will let you create content that they can connect more with, this will build a more loyal following.

Consider the following pointers:

- **Demographics** – What is the age, gender and location of your ideal viewer? This will let you target them specifically.

- **Interests** – What are their hobbies, passions or preferences? By understanding this, you can offer videos that cater to their tastes and deliver value on them.

- **Challenges** – Do they face any challenges, problems or obstacles? If you address these or provide content that solves problems, such as tutorials for common issues, you can become a trusted resource for them.

Forming a Unique & Consistent Brand

If you want to set yourself apart from the competition, you need to stand out. Your branding is everything, it's the combined package consisting of the visual, verbal and emotional elements you deliver; how you present yourself and speak on camera, the value you deliver and the emotional response you instill in the viewer.

A personal brand is the most powerful on YouTube. Many choose not to show their face, and I did for a long time at the beginning, but showing your face (be it with a face cam in the corner in a gaming video or a full face camera for personal content) will allow you to connect more with the viewer. There's millions of YouTubers, and most of them don't show their face, if you're a commentary channel, do you want to be another of the million channels with only a voice? Exactly… you're not memorable, if you don't upload, they'll forget you, you won't be missed. Nobody will know much about you, nobody can connect with you, you're replaceable, the next trend comes and you're gone. Be irreplaceable, connect to your audience.

A personal brand will also let you sell products and make more money, because there's something about trusting a real person with a face that can be connected to the voice. Try selling products or services or promoting anything with a faceless channel, believe me… it doesn't work. This will hurt you later if you want to go full time.

So let's consider the following:

- **Visual Identity** – Choose your own color scheme, font, and logo that represents your channel's personality and tone. Try to keep your visuals consistent across your channel art, your thumbnails, and video overlays.

- **Channel Name** – This should be short, snappy and memorable. It should be simple to pronounce and represent yourself, your niche and brand personality.

- **Tone & Voice** – Develop a consistent tone and voice for your channel. This will include precisely how you speak in your videos, your content style, and how you interact with your audience. Your tone and voice should remain authentic and relatable, helping to build a connection with your viewers.

I'm mostly known for my Minecraft mods videos and Top 10 style videos. I use the same thumbnail styles, around 2 or 3, across all of my content in this sub-niche, so people know and recognize an upload by thebluecrusader, my channel. Many have emulated and copied my video format, thumbnail style and brand identity over the years, most to no success, some to great success, but emulation is simply flattery, it's a complement. However, emulating and copying another creator is not creating your own brand and it will not work in the long term, you must create your own package and brand to stand out, YouTube is only oversaturated because everyone is trying to be the same as their competitors in their chosen niche.

By carefully forming your foundation, you'll stand out, resonate with your audience and set yourself on a path to success.

Creating Compelling Content

Now that you've taken time to lay that solid foundation for your vision, it's time to begin the good part… Creating compelling content is EVERYTHING. This is going to be the backbone of your YouTube success. I'm going to be honest with you, it doesn't matter if you read all of this chapter, if you're a total beginner, you're going to have to put in the hours to learn to create good content, hundreds, maybe thousands of hours to perfect it, it's a forever process.

I'm going to talk to you about the art of storytelling, and we'll take a look at various different formats and styles of video and I'll share some sauce on the scripting and planning side of your video creation process. If you can master such elements, you will be able to attract viewers, retain them and bring them back.

The Art of Storytelling

The most essential part of creating videos that are both engaging and memorable is by mastering storytelling. It really does not matter what your niche is, you still should try to implement some kind of story. Humans are tribal creatures, and telling stories are how we connect with each other. If you want to connect with your audience on that deeper level, you must become a skilled storyteller, meaning you must:

- **Hook Them** – Begin each video with a captivating hook that grabs your viewer's attention and entices them to continue watching by teasing the value early, in the form of a question, a bold statement or a preview of what's to come, and then deliver on that promise later in the video.

- **Structure Your Story** – Every good story that has been told has a structure, a beginning, a middle and an ending. If you want your story to flow in a logical manner and have a sense of purpose and direction, try to keep to this.

- **Use Emotion** – Play on the viewer's emotion. This works especially well with a personal brand channel when you share your personal or past experiences, tell stories from your life and show vulnerability, make them laugh, make them curious or invoke excitement. This also works in viral videos like when MrBeast donates to homeless people for example.

Video Formats & Style

There's a whole bunch of different formats and styles out there for you to choose from and many are dependent on your chosen niche and target audience. Experimenting with some of these varying formats can help you along the way to figure out the best way that you can convey your message and showcase your unique personality to connect with others. A few examples of video formats you can experiment with are:

- **Tutorials & How to's** – You teach the viewer a new skill or walk them through a task in a step by step process, you're directly providing value by solving problems.

- **Vlogs** – By showing your life, your experiences or behind the scenes, you're really connecting with your audience on a personal level.

- **Reviews** – Share your opinions on products and services to help viewers come to a conclusion. This type builds big trust and establishes you as a figure of authority, it also has big opportunities later down the line for sponsorships from companies who will pay you for a product feature, a review or send you free products.

- **Lists Videos** – You create an interesting or informative video such as a "Top 5" list or fact video based on your niche or desired topic.

- **Video Essay** – A commentary style video based on a video script on a certain topic, easy to incorporate story telling.

Scripting & Planning

Most of my videos on my main gaming channel are commentary style videos, many being Top 10 list videos, some being faceless reviews or documentary style videos and narration format content. Because of this, I have a lot of experience, thousands of hours, in writing scripts for both film and YouTube. Having a well-structured script for a video will significantly improve both the quality of your content and speed up the process of the video production. If you have a script or a set of notes, you won't be rambling, so the video will be more to the point, which improves the viewer experience.

- **Form an Outline** – Before you begin writing your script, you should form an outline for the main points you're going to cover, this will give you an idea of the flow you will be keeping and following, you can begin by adding chapter headings and notes or just writing bullet points before you begin writing.

- **Forming Detail** – A script will make it easier to keep organization, remove those annoying repetitive or filler words and mistakes. If you're reading a script fully, try to practice your speaking and presentation skills, or if you're using bullet points as prompts, try to use them only as queues, both of these habits will help you to sound less like a robot or unnatural.

- **Envision the Visuals** – Think about the visuals you're going to use to support the content, such as the on-screen text, graphics or B-roll or stock footage. Planning your visuals in advance and adding them in as script notes will make your editing process in post much easier and efficient.

- **Rehearse** - Before you begin recording, think about practicing your script and your delivery a bunch of times. This will let you become more comfortable on camera, you may even need to do a whole lot of takes until you get it right. But, if you're totally new, you're just going to have to make videos and be ok with putting them out there, it's trial by fire, you only learn by doing.

Storytelling is an art you must master. Even if you need to experiment with multiple formats and styles, becoming adept at these skills will propel you to success.

Mastering the YouTube Algorithm

Understanding how YouTube's algorithm is just as important as knowing how to deliver compelling content. If you're clueless on how to package and deliver it, you could create the best video in the world and absolutely nobody will see it, ever…

I'm going to reveal the secrets behind the YouTube algorithm, as it currently stands. I learnt some of this information by doing, some by studying, and the majority from an actual YouTube employee from the search and discovery team! Yes, that means he WORKS on the algorithm! This is insider information…

The New Algorithm Revealed

The elusive YouTube Algorithm... People make it way more complex than it genuinely is. I've got videos over 1 million views, I know how it works and how to play it, but it really isn't as multi-tiered and confusing as you think it is.

In fact, the YouTube Algorithm isn't some matrix that's hard to comprehend and game, it's simple. YouTube surfaces videos to relevant audiences based on their personal viewing behavior, such as the things they watch (and don't watch) and search for. It ranks your videos you upload against all other videos that the viewer may watch, and its performance may be influenced by differences in audiences.

Also, hear this; recommendations depend on the user's behavior, not just on YouTube, but also Google and... CHROME! (Yes the browser), bet you didn't know that...

To put it simply, make good videos. Yes, that's it. Long gone are the days of using clickbait to lure in a viewer. If they don't watch the video long after, and click off, guess what? YouTube isn't pushing your video. You want success? Focus on making GOOD VIDEOS!

Here's some key factors you can focus on for maximizing your success with the YouTube Algorithm:

- **Appeal** – Impressions & Click-through rate (aka CTR) is very crucial in understanding the percentage of impressions that turned into views. You can improve this metric by optimizing your

thumbnails and creating better and more clickable titles that represent your video content.
- **Engagement** – Analyze your best performing videos to understand what are the factors that made them successful and build upon that for your future content to replicate the success. Optimize your thumbnails to make sure your videos stand out in the search results, recommended videos and on the home page. Depending where they show up of course.
- **Satisfaction** – Add your video content to playlists, use end screens to point to more related content at the end, and check the consistency of your titles and thumbnails. Experiment with new topics and formats, and engage with your audience to understand what they wish to see from you in the future.
- **Value** – Focus on providing value to your audience, both in terms of information and the entertainment factor. In business, you get paid in relation to the value you provide and lives you change, this is no different in YouTube success (and money). Encourage those that aren't subscribed to subscribe – you can do this by using the end screens and call-to-actions in your script, and then promote your other videos on the end screens too!

The most important factors to conquer the algorithm are improving your click-through rate to get viewers to first click, then achieve high-audience retention (watch time) by having well-paced, engaging editing and commentary and watch as your video succeeds, it's as simple as those two metrics.

YouTube Analytics: Your Secret Weapon

Your greatest weapon for optimizing your content, doing market research to analyze competitors, see the performance of your videos and channel as a whole and generally monitor your progress and strategy is the YouTube Creator Studio's Analytics section. You can use this to:

- Check the number of subscribers who turned on "All Notifications" for your channel and enabled YouTube notifications. You can do a call to action and visual prompt in your video editing to remind them to enable notifications.
- Consider what times your viewers are most active on YouTube and then modify your upload schedule accordingly to post your videos at the most optimal times to gain momentum and views from early birds.
- Analyze your video performance and identify patterns and trends that contribute to your success. Use this information to inform your future content strategy.

A long with the YouTube Analytics feature, you can also refer to YouTube's resources, like their official Creator channel on YouTube and their articles, for some more tips on increasing views and improving your channel's performance.

By mastering the YouTube Algorithm and focusing upon the main key factors of appeal, engagement, satisfaction, and value, you'll be on your way to maximize your chance of visibility for your videos and seeing channel growth.

SEO: Thumbnails, Titles & Tags

Ok, so now you've got the main part out of the way, the content creation. However, I'm sorry to tell you, but that's actually only half of the battle. After you learn how to create good and engaging videos, you need to learn what's called "SEO", this means "Search Engine Optimization", think of this like marketing – this will help people find your videos. This encapsulates everything: thumbnails, titles AND tags.

Crafting Eye-Catching Thumbnails

When creating your perfect little package for your video, the thumbnail is the most important visual element, this is the very first thing viewers are going to see as soon as they come across your content, in the search, on the home page or in the recommended videos box on the side bar.

Having an eye-catching thumbnail is going to be the main driving factor to significantly increase your click-through rate and magnetize more viewers to watch your content. Creating the compelling thumbnails though requires the following:

- **Use High Quality Images** – Ensure that your thumbnail is sharp and clear. Don't use pixelated or low quality graphics or images, avoid this!

- **Utilize Bold Colors & Contrasts** – Try to use colors that stand out and contrast well with each other to grab the viewer's attention. I've found personally that very bright colors, like the colors of the rainbow, work very well – particularly bright blue, bright yellow and white. These work universally, but your choices may change based on the age and niche of the viewers you're targeting.
- **Have Clear & Concise Text** – Make sure the text you use in your thumbnail is extremely clear, this means it needs to be legible! i.e EASY to read, even on smaller screens.
- **Use Human Faces** – If you have a personal brand channel in which you show your face, this one is easy. If not, perhaps you can't do this. But typically using faces in your thumbnails work very well, it also makes them more relatable, engaging and you can use faces and expressions to convey emotion and express the tone of your content.
- **Have Consistent Branding** – Your thumbnails should align with your overall channel's branding to create a cohesive and professional appearance that people remember you for, this could be different for certain series or types of videos you have, but try to retain a core style people know you for.

Writing Compelling Titles

A long with a good thumbnail, a great title is crucial for attracting those viewers and improving the searchability of your video. Think of it likes this… When you see a news article, what makes you click one of them, and what makes you not click the other? Usually the title…

Now listen, the title can utilize some click-bait, but do NOT oversell it, or overdo it. Also it needs to be just enticing enough to acquire the viewer's trust to click it, but the video has to deliver the promise of the title. If the title is misleading to the video, they will click off, then your viewer retention will suck and your video won't get pushed.

Keep some of this in mind:

- **Be Descriptive but Accurate:** Your title needs to accurately represent the video's content and give a clear idea of what's to expect when someone watches it.
- **Use relevant keywords:** Incorporate popular and relevant keywords related to your videos topic to improve searchability so people can find it. But, try to avoid stuffing tons of keywords in to the title or using misleading ones, this will harm any kind of credibility you have or haven't yet built and can also result in penalties by violating YouTube's terms of service, this is the same for tags too.
- **Be Concise:** Aim to keep titles to around 60 characters or less, longer titles will get shortened or cut off on devices like mobiles and tablets.

- **Evoke curiosity:** Make use of your title to try to spark some kind of interest and some curiosity without having to resort to making use of egregious clickbait tactics. Like I said before, you have to deliver on the promise made in your title, so don't set yourself up for failure by lying or misleading people.

Mastering Tags & Optimization

Tags are no longer as important as they once were. However, don't believe the biggest of YouTubers who mislead you into believing tags are meaningless and useless (sorry MrBeast). Most of these YouTubers have already gone viral and YouTube are pushing their videos on the home page already, so they don't need tags. BUT, I bet they made good use of them in the beginning.

Tags, along with your title and description, feed YouTube and its algorithm some information to understand what your video's content is all about, helping to rank it accordingly.

You can use the "research tab" in the Creator Studio's Analytics section to search for keywords to see what's popular and use them in your titles & descriptions and in your tags.

Follow some of these best practices:

- **Use relevant tags:** Choose a list of tags that best represent what your video actually is and the content, and use tags relevant to your target audience and what they're searching for. Try to make use of a mix of broad and specific tags.

- **Avoid Overuse –** Don't use too many tags. Now, it's best to use the full characters available, but don't overdo it if you haven't got any more to put in there. Too many tags may dilute the focus if you put unrelated tags in there to fill up the limit.
- **Use Keyword Tools –** As stated before, YouTube has a free keyword research tool in the Creator Studio's Analytics section called the Research Tab. However, there's third-party keyword research tools that help identify popular and trending keywords, and these are very powerful, I'll link you to the best two that I use below:

TubeBuddy – https://www.tubebuddy.com/dean

VidIQ - https://vidiq.com/dean

- **Include Your Channel Name:** If you add in your channel name as a tag, this can help improve your video's visibility. I started doing this early, and it helped my existing fans or past viewers who hadn't subscribed, actually find my videos. Also sometimes when they type in a keyword related to your channel, it'll show your channel name in the search box, peaking interest of new viewers, giving you some form of social proof.

If you can understand how to optimize your thumbnails, your video's titles, and the tags you choose to use, you can really improve your video's discoverability. This will help you attract more viewers, and increase your chances of success on YouTube's saturated ecosystem.

Fostering a Loyal, Engaged Community

As a YouTube creator, what is paramount to your success is the community that stands behind you and your content. This is one of the biggest key factors in your success. You MUST cultivate a loyal and engaged audience. A dedicated community that roots for you not only boosts your channel's visibility through the engagement (the likes, comments, and shares), but also fosters a sense of belonging and connection to your audience, and eliminates that whole imposter syndrome sense that so many suffer from.

Engaging with Your Audience

If you want to create that deeper sense of connection and encourage your viewers to come back for more and become a regular, you must engage with them, and do it actively and effectively. Consider the following fundamentals:

- **Respond to comments:** You should absolutely take the time to individually read and respond to each and every comment on your videos, especially in the beginning when there isn't too many to keep on top of. Engaging in conversations with your viewers will make them feel heard and appreciated, which strengthens their connection to you and your channel. I make it a core principle to reply to each and every one of my viewers on my new videos, there's still a backlog of thousands of comments on my older videos I can't keep up with though, but this is the dark truth of having nearly 2,000 videos that keep getting new comments… My fans are shocked that someone with 100,000 subscribers is actually taking the time to actively reply and have conversations with them, it really sets you apart, because so many YouTubers neglect their core supporters, be different.

- **Ask for Feedback:** You can further encourage those viewers to share their thoughts and opinions on your content. This is great free market research that will let you get some feedback on how you can improve and demonstrate you value their input by making changes accordingly or using their ideas for videos. I use the YouTube channel "Community" tab for this. I do regular posts with questions to see what people want to see in future videos and I do monthly polls to get data on what they like the most of what I've been putting out. Use this with analytics to get a full picture.
- **Host Q&As:** If you do livestreams, it can be really powerful to do a Q&A session or answer any questions live. This is super personal because you're answering in real time and really connecting to your audience.

Leveraging Social Media

If you want to further broker a connection to your fans and your audience, you can make use of the many other social media platforms already out there. However, long gone are the times that you can easily retweet your videos and get easy engagement, that was already dying out in 2015 when I was doing it, trust me. If you want to solely use socials for promotion, you're going to have to clever now, and that may involve some "questionable" tactics such as being highly controversial, which I don't recommend.

But, platforms like Instagram, Facebook & Twitter can be a great place to engage with your viewers or repost your content on, such as shorts (short form content), to reach a wider audience, multi-platform. However, I don't use Twitter personally, it's a cesspit for toxicity, I merely lurk on there semi-rarely.

- **Choose the right platforms:** You should try to focus on the social media platforms that best suit your target audience and the niche of your content you chose earlier. Popular ones are of course Instagram, Twitter, Facebook, and TikTok, but not all of them may be easy to get into or may appeal to you.
- **Share exclusive content** – To increase the engagement on your other social media channels, you can share exclusive videos, clips, or content of some form. This could be behind-the-scenes videos, exclusive updates, or teasers for upcoming videos.
- **Engage with your fans** – Just like with YouTube, you should also engage with your fans

on the other platforms too, that means make sure to respond to comments, messages, tweets or social media mentions to create a more personal connection.
- **Cross Promotion** – You can use these sites to promote your content. Like I said before, Twitter is kind of oversaturated, and so is Facebook, but using Instagram reels and TikTok to reshare your short form content you posted on YouTube shorts can bring extra traffic to your channel fairly easily.

Collaborations

Listen, I'm not speaking from experience in this part. In fact, I'm going to be frankly honest with you, I've never had a collaboration with another creator, that is if you don't count my friends from my videos who don't even have their own YouTube channels…

In fact, I've never had any kind of shoutout, collab, or help or assist, and that's greatly hurt my growth and made it slow!

But, it definitely felt much better being "self-made" … But I can tell you, if the opportunity had come up, I would have taken it.

Nobody bigger than you is going to give you a shoutout or do a collab, no matter how many times you spam in their comments or DMs.

The dark truth about YouTube collabs is it's a value exchange; meaning, what can you do for me? You don't have more subscribers? Forget it… You can't help me make viral content or pay me large sums of money? Forget it... That's not my talking, that's every big YouTuber (secretly), they won't admit it... ever.

BUT, if you can find someone at a similar level, or a little smaller, or someone a tiny bit bigger, who is willing to collab with you, it can be POWERFUL.

Creating content with other YouTubers can help you tap into a whole new audience, you're theoretically sharing each other's audiences with eachother, so be sure to make a good first impression.

Here's some food for thought:

- **Choose relevant partners** – Try to collaborate with those YouTube Creators who wield a similar type of target audience or are in the same type of content niche. If you're a gamer, and they're a beauty girl, it probably won't work, unless. you're super super clever with it. This means you're ensuring both your audiences are in-line with each other and there's mass appeal.
- **Plan Thoroughly** – You should do some behind-the-scenes work first, get to the drawing board. You need to develop a clear concept, outline, and maybe a script if needed, for the video and how you're going to make it work.
- **Cross-Promote** – If you share the video/s on both of your channels and social medias and leverage the right promotional features, you'll make sure to maximize the visibility and reach across both your social followings, so the videos get the best chance of success.

Through engagement, leveraging your socials and collaborating, you're on the way to build a strong engaged community.

Monetizing Your YouTube Machine

For those uninitiated, this chapter is all about the shiny stuff, MONEY!

Ok, so now that I've got your interest, let's talk.

So you've got past the lecture on building your community of loyal and engaged followers. Perhaps, you're reading this later, and you've found some growth, perhaps you're just planning ahead. Well, the next part would be to consider monetization strategies... Monetizing your channel is going to provide you with the financial means to invest in higher-quality content, better equipment, and turn your YouTube passion into a full-time gig, aka a job!

YouTube's Partner Program

The YouTube Partner Program (YPP) is the main way that you're going to be able to make money... This is the way in which you're going to be able to get direct revenue from your videos through the means of YouTube ads, BUT, you actually need to meet some requirements to get initiated, which are:

- At least 1,000 Subscribers
- At least 4,000 hours of watch time across your videos in the last 12 months

You must meet these requirements to get enrolled and accepted so that you can begin making money with ad placements upon your videos, as well as YouTube Premium revenue, and access to livestream donations or "Super Chats" as they're called. Later, you can enable merch, to sell shirts, although these are very hard to sell.

Remember we picked a niche earlier? Well your niche actually matters when it comes to making money from ads. Unfortunately for me, I had no clue about this... I followed by passion as a teenager for playing games and now I have a successful gaming channel, which is nice... But I'm not a millionaire, as gaming pays the lowest out of all categories! I don't do bad though...

But what makes the most you ask? Anything that relates to money, products like tech, or in industries that have a lot of cash flow or investment or highly profitable businesses.

Remember when I said think twice about following your passion? If you choose a niche that pays higher, you'll not need to work for as many views to stay afloat.

Affiliate Marketing

One option to monetize your content way before you even get accepted into the partner program is through affiliate marketing.

What on earth is that? Well, it's basically a means of making money by promoting other companies' products or services. You sign up for a so-called "affiliate program" and use your special referral link, and when people sign up with it or make a purchase, you get a percentage of the profit as a commission. This does require some effort and a lot of sales to make a sizeable amount however.

I'd recommend Amazon's "Amazon Associates" affiliate program. It's the most accessible, trust worthy and they're already an established brand everyone trusts, so if you advertise Amazon products, you don't also need to learn how to sell, because people already know, like and trust Amazon as a business.

Think about this:

- **Pick relevant products** – Try to seek out products and services that are relevant to your content's niche or that your audience would genuinely find beneficial to their life or valuable in some way, remember, our goal is always to deliver value to our audience and help them. If you want to make money, you need to first serve the customer or your audience and help them in exchange for the reward, in this case money.
- **Disclose your affiliation** – Make sure to put in your video description that you're using affiliate links so people know you're making a commission on the links, people love transparency, always be honest.
- **Create valuable content** – Remember, valuable content will build trust with your core fans and if its related to the products or services you're promoting, it'll build natural interest and require minimal sales to try to promote what you're selling.

Sponsored Content

One great thing about creating a personal brand or generally just a YouTube channel is the prospect of partnering with your favorite brands. Every week I get emails to work with cool companies and advertise their products or software. But, I only actually take a fraction of these opportunities, and I'll tell you why in a moment…

Your growth will attract companies who want to tap into your social media audience and presence to drive traffic or sales to their products and services and they'll pay you to make them a video or feature their products in yours.

But, you should always maintain your core values. One thing that's kept me relevant and successful on YouTube is never promoting snake-oil (scams or bad products) to my audience and always having their best interests in mind. I've been offered hundreds or thousands to promote shady gambling websites or degenerative companies and I've turned every single one down, even the grey-area ones like seemingly fun crypto games. Anything I can't prove is safe, secure or legit, I decline immediately, I don't want to hurt my audience. My lesson to you, NEVER accept a quick buck in exchange to hurt your audience, they are your backbone, they are why you're successful, never betray their trust for dirty money.

So, for sponsorships, let's consider this:

- **Be Classy** – Present your channel and brand professionally, keep that consistent branding, the high quality content and an engaged audience to retain your high market value and to stay attractive to sponsors.
- **Pitch to Brands** – Reach out when possible to brands within your content niche that align to

your target audience and their values, work with brands that match your channels mission.
- **Be transparent** – Always disclose in the video, the video's description, and in the video options (you can enable a tick box that shows on the video to the viewers that it contains paid promotion) to show that your video is sponsored, this is so they can identify if it is slightly biased or has an underlying motive so they can not feel deceived, this helps to maintain that trust, because once it's lost, it's lost forever.
- **Don't Sell Out** – If you think a brand or sponsorship is untrustworthy, shady, or something universally frowned upon or disliked, don't become a "shill" and sell-out by promoting a poor product or service for quick money, this is a cardinal YouTube sin, don't do this, nobody will respect you.

Selling Merchandise

Now, merchandise is kind of a love-hate relationship for me. Look, I'll be honest, I haven't been personally successful selling t-shirts, and I made a pretty cool shirt collection. Want to know why? The margins are terrible... And so is the pricing. To put it simply, if you want to make it easy, you'll work with YouTube's merch partners, they'll take a cut and handle the shipping. But, you receive a small fraction of the sale price and the products are extremely expensive for your audience, who most likely won't buy it unless you're a mega star or have a VERY strong personal brand. But, if you decide to go down this path least-travelled, let me share some wisdom:

- **Design unique & appealing products** – Look, if you want to stand out, your products need to

reflect your branding and it MUST appeal to your audience. And it must have some kind of wow-factor or be something unique that's not been seen before, or have a super cool quote…
- **Picking Reliable Suppliers –** Honestly, YouTube has partners you can use from YouTube Studio under the "Shopping" section, it's super easy to set up. But if you want good profit and a better business, you need to find a supplier. But, this requires setting up a real business, I don't have enough experience in this to guide you. But, you can start with the website "Alibaba".
- **Promotion –** To drive sales, you need to do call-to-actions in your video to tell your viewers to make a purchase on your store, it'll also show below your videos on the "merch shelf" which shows your merchandise to people watching so they can click and buy.
-

By diversifying your income streams and implementing some of these various strategies to monetize your channel, you can turn your YouTube dream into a profitable business venture.

As I mentioned before, this is going to be a whole lot easier if you pick a niche that is based on an industry that has a lot of money. If you make business videos, your ads will pay well, your audience will most likely actually have money to buy your products and you'll have it easy when you finally get big on YouTube.

The Long-Term Growth Strategy

If you thought achieving the initial growth on YouTube was a grandeur task, then be prepared for the incredible accomplishment of maintaining long-term growth and sustainability, that requires ongoing effort and adaptability.

Just like the "passive income" lie, in which people claim you can be lazy and sit back and make thousands of dollars on auto-pilot, YouTube is the same. You can't sit and let your channel make your passive money for weeks on end, or it will slowly suffocate in the algorithm. You need to upload at least once a week or every two weeks to not experience a down trend from inactivity.

Adapting to Change

The YouTube landscape is constantly evolving, with all new trends, algorithm changes, and platform updates. You should be staying informed with any changes if you want long-term success. When the site changes, gets updates, or the algorithm gets altered, it can affect you and your new business.

- **Follow news** – If you can, subscribe to any YouTube growth channels, newsletters focused on the topic or websites that post news articles or update you with trends to keep informed.
- **Join Communities** – If you join some communities for new creators, you'll be exposed

to all new insights, second hand experiences and advice from already established creators. You can do this on forums, social media groups, Discord serves or subreddits.

Consistently Producing High Quality Content

Listen, if you got the ball rolling, there's no slowing down now… That is, if you don't want to get eaten alive and spat out into irrelevancy.

Consistency is key in terms of maintaining this growth ball you've managed to accumulate and if you want to keep the snowball expanding, you should keep posting great videos your audience loves, keep some form of schedule and keep those fans loyal. Remember, you're replaceable, and if you aren't showing your face or building any kind of genuine connection, you're old news if you get lazy.

- **Develop a content calendar** – Try to plan your content in advance ahead of time, before you create it. This will let you make a schedule to keep your content creation process efficient and streamlined, meaning keeping consistency and staying organized is always simple.
- **Batch produce content** – If you have some time on your hands, go ahead and produce multiple videos all at once to save a bunch of time and ensure you have fresh content always ready to make and upload. Gaming videos are so easy to do this, you can see how I put out 4 videos a day for a year or two now back in the day right? For my content nowadays, the more scripted, higher quality stuff, I make use of batch recording voice overs for scripts I've already batch-written, so I

have a ton of video narrations to edit into full videos, you get the idea…
- **Optimize your workflow –** If you start making money, or you already have a job, invest both your time and your money into tools and software that save you lots of time. Half of my monthly expenses are on the tools I mentioned above for keyword research, "VidIQ" and "TubeBuddy", as well as a whole roster of A.I tools, these all help me stay ahead of 99% of people in the YouTube game, both in quality and frequency.

Analyzing Performance & Adjusting Accordingly

Listen, you've always got to stay on top of your game. You NEED to always be looking how your channel and its content is performing in order to be up to date. You should regularly be in the YouTube analytics to see what's working and identify those areas that need improvement.

Consider these key metrics:

- **Watch time**
- **Audience retention**
- **Click-through rate**
- **Subscriber growth**
- **Engagement (Likes, Comments, Shares)**

If you can focus on monitoring all of these, you can easily see which types of content you've been posting that is really resonating with your audience the most and try to use this data to make more informed decisions about future video topics, formats, and strategies for promoting your content.

Diversifying Your Content

Listen, I'm going to lament over this note again in case you didn't pay attention to me earlier... You should be expanding your content outreach to other platforms available to you if you want to succeed and promote growth.

You should be considering the potential of branching out to experiment with some different video formats, collaborating with any creators in your circle or that are accessible to you, or even launching some kind of third-party venture that will supplement or complement your YouTube content, like a podcast or second channel, which may be better later when you're established so that you don't split too much into your time.

Expanding Beyond YouTube

Think of YouTube as your main bread and butter, but that doesn't mean you can't grow a pair of wings and leave the nest. Reflecting on your expansion beyond YouTube as a sole platform can be beneficial, mainly because you can diversify your online presence and venture into all new opportunities, reach new audiences, strengthen that brand identity and integrity you've worked so hard to build, and create even more additional revenue streams to monetize outside of YouTube.

Launching a Website or Blog

A really powerful way to market yourself if you have a personal brand channel, is to create some kind of personal website, in the form of a blog or portfolio. This can also house any products you may sell later, like online courses, digital products like books etc.

- **Website Builders –** There's a bunch of good website builders, but a few trusted ones would be WordPress (which I use), Wix & Squarespace – which also can create very professional looking sites.
- **Engaging Content –** If you write blog articles, you can complement your videos by writing within the same topic, embedding/including your video in the article too.

- **Optimize for Search Engines** – As we did with SEO earlier in this book, you should try to utilize some of these same strategies on your website to make sure your website has the best chance to show up when someone has a Google search.

The Art of Podcasting

Long form content has almost seen a resurgence again recently, perhaps due in fact to the litter of short form content we've seen in the last year.

Because of this, podcasts, particularly ones in video form, are massively popular. Launching a podcast is one of the most powerful ways to reach new audiences and provide a unique platform to discuss in-depth topics.

The reason this is SO POWERFUL is because of "social hacking". Social hacking has always been a thing on YouTube. In plain terms, it's using someone's name for clout or views, you're tapping into someone who is already established and using the interest of their fan base to get views on your videos on them or about them, it's a good strategy for growth when you're a nobody.

With podcasts, you can get guests regularly and tap into all of their audiences and see exponential growth.

- **Pick a good topic** – Choose a podcast theme that aligns with the content you're already making and appeal to your target audience.
- **Invest in quality equipment** – If you want to run a podcast, you need to get a good quality microphone and recording software to make sure your audio and podcast is going to bring the best experience possible.

- **Promotion** – Try to share your podcasts on your YouTube, as well as your other socials and your site (if you made it) to reach a wider audience.

Livestreaming

Live streaming is also an interest forte to break into. Sure, there's Twitch and Facebook Live, but YouTube's live service is all built in to your channel already, so why not tap into it?

Like we mentioned earlier, you can really connect with your audience on a deeper level when you're on camera in real time talking to them, like you're in the room with them, this is the more interactive of content you can produce.

- **Schedule regular streams** – If you choose to stream, try to host regular streams to make sure everyone stays engaged and build upon their anticipation to deliver exciting entertaining live experiences.
- **Promotion** – You can announce the streams on your YouTube channel's community tab and your socials and site to attract viewers in.
- **Engagement** – Try your best to stay on top of comments, donations and viewers talking to you live so you can resonate with them.

Overcoming Challenges

Now that you've discovered how to start, how to grow and how to conquer the platform, it's time we had a sit down and I taught you about how to face the challenges you're going to run into. Listen, you're going to have A LOT of setbacks. You NEED resilience, you need to learn from these experiences, and STAY MOTIVATED. The last is the most important, it took me TWO YEARS to see big success on YouTube and I'm only at 100,000 subscribers, there's still 1 million as a milestone…

Handling Criticism

When you put yourself out there online, criticism, negative feedback and even actual hatred are unavoidable. But, it'll give you a tough skin. This game isn't for the faint-hearted. If you're a snowflake or if it'll trigger you, you're not cut out for it.

In fact, I'm going to give you my strategy to deflect negativity, handle situations constructively and diffuse the toxicity.

- **Separate constructive from destructive criticism –** You must learn to recognize constructive criticism that is aimed to help you improve, and disregard unfounded negative comments that serve no purpose. The key is how they're written, negative comments don't point

out the specific issue, rather just spew hatred at you.
- **Develop a support network** – If you have a good friendship circle, it'll be easier, especially if you have YouTuber friends and family who can keep you going with encouragement and support during these challenges. I never had YouTuber friends, never did collabs, but the bad comments helped me a lot.
- **Focus on the positive** – Realize that most hate comments come from personal suffering, most of the time someone is just having a bad day and you triggered them or made them feel lesser by something you did. Perhaps you smiled, and they wish they were feeling that way, maybe they're jealous of what you have. Always respond kindly. 90% of hate comments can be diffused with kindness, or simply saying "Are you ok?", or replying with a joke or light-heartedness. The majority of the time they'll apologize or explain why they did what they did, sometimes they had a bad day, just wanted to be noticed or felt a certain way in the moment. Those that don't back down, you can block them from your channel, don't respond harshly, they may be having a horrible time in their life.

Creative Burnout

At some point, you're going to reach the dreaded "Creative Burnout", but, if you position yourself well, you can avoid it.

If you get this feeling, you either posted too much content and need a break, or you're making videos you no longer enjoy to make. I am the type to get depressed if I'm not creating or working.

Every time I got creative burnout, it was from either falling out of love with the videos I was making, or from over posting with little growth in return (meaning I felt undervalued).

If I ever burnout now, I change my videos, I post what I WANT, and then I ride the wave and chose to either return to the older videos or change my niche or format and welcome a new audience. Don't betray yourself or your own interests to please your audience if it makes you depressed, burnt-out or fall out of love with what you loved.

Conclusion

Throughout this book, I've shared with you many of my personal strategies and the insights I've made use of to build my YouTube channel into a success from the ground up.

As you now embark on your own YouTube adventure, I'm excited to see what progress you make. Remember that the key for your everlasting success is staying true to what you're good at or interested in and consistently delivering value to your audience.

Success is no overnight achievement, it will take months, years. Some of the biggest creators were nothing until years of work paid off. If you think in days or weeks and don't have a long term time horizon for the future, you will fail.

By having a growth mindset and following my core principles then you'll be way on your way to achieve the success you've been dreaming about.

Never forget the power that your unique voice has and the potential impact that your content will have on your audience. Embrace the challenges bestowed upon you, celebrate your victories, and enjoy the incredible journey of becoming a successful YouTuber.

www.ingramcontent.com/pod-product-compliance
Lightning Source LLC
LaVergne TN
LVHW051621050326
832903LV00033B/4609